Quiet Success: An Introvert's Guide to Thriving in Real Estate

Table of Contents

INTRODUCTION

The Quiet Power in Real Estate

In the high-octane world of real estate, where networking events buzz with activity and negotiations echo with energetic banter, it's easy to assume that success is reserved for the loudest voice in the room. However, beneath the surface, a different force thrives, often going unnoticed but making an impact that's deep and lasting – the introvert.

The Unique Strengths of Introverts in Real Estate

Introverts, by nature, process the world differently. While they might shy away from the limelight, their strengths lie in observation, deep thinking, and genuine connection. In real estate, this translates to:

1. Deep Relationships: An introvert's ability to foster deep, meaningful relationships ensures trust and loyalty from clients. It's not about the number of hands shaken at an event, but the depth of the handshake, the quality of conversation, and the sincerity of the follow-up.

2. Attention to Detail: In a market where details can make or break a deal, the introverted agent's propensity for analysis and reflection is invaluable. They catch nuances others might overlook, from clauses in contracts to subtle shifts in a client's preferences.

3. Empathetic Negotiation: Introverts are keen listeners. This allows them to understand the unsaid needs and concerns of clients, leading to negotiations that are rooted in empathy, ensuring a win-win for all parties involved.

4. Strategic Planning: Instead of shooting in the dark, introverts in real estate tend to approach their tasks with a well-thought-out strategy. They ponder over market trends, anticipate changes, and are always a step ahead.

Dispelling the Myth: Real Estate Isn't Just for Extroverts

The real estate world is rife with the myth that only extroverted personalities can thrive. This couldn't be further from the truth. While extroverts have their own set of strengths, introverts bring a different, equally valuable set of skills to the table. The industry, vast and varied as it is, has room for all personality types.

Moreover, the landscape of real estate is changing. With the digital era, many traditional processes are shifting online, giving introverts more platforms where they naturally excel. Virtual home tours, email campaigns, and online consultations cater to the strengths of the introvert, highlighting that success in real estate isn't about being the loudest, but about being the most effective.

This book aims to shine a light on the power of introversion in the real estate industry. It is an invitation to all the introverted real estate enthusiasts to embrace their unique qualities, to dispel misconceived notions, and to understand that in the orchestra of real estate, it's not always the loudest instruments that make the most profound impact. Sometimes, it's the quiet ones that linger and resonate long after the last note is played.

Chapter 1:

Embracing Your Inner Introvert

Navigating the bustling world of real estate as an introvert can feel like trying to swim upstream. The environment seems dominated by the extroverted: the charismatic negotiators, the loud networkers, and the gregarious salespeople. I know this all too well, as I have walked this path myself. Here's a dive into some personal challenges I faced and how embracing the inner introvert can turn the tide in your favor.

Recognizing Your Introverted Qualities

The first step is acknowledging that being an introvert isn't a weakness. It's just a different way of experiencing the world. Here were some telltale signs I identified in my journey:

1. Energy Drain in Large Gatherings: After attending open houses or networking events, I felt drained, craving some quiet time to recharge. While many colleagues seemed to gain energy from these gatherings, I felt the opposite.

2. Deep Thinker: Rather than making decisions on the fly, I always preferred taking time to ponder, analyze, and come to a well-informed decision.

3. Listening over Talking: During client meetings or discussions with colleagues, I realized I was more

comfortable listening and absorbing information rather than dominating the conversation.

4. Preference for One-on-One: Instead of big group meetings, I was more effective and comfortable in one-on-one settings or with smaller groups.

Understanding the Value You Bring to the Real Estate Industry

It took time, but I came to realize that being an introvert wasn't a barrier but rather a unique advantage. Here's how:

1. Deep Connections: While I might not have been the life of the party at networking events, the few connections I did make were deep and meaningful. Clients I worked with appreciated the genuine interest I showed in their needs, translating to long-term relationships.

2. Attention to Detail: My tendency to introspect and analyze served well when assessing property values, understanding market trends, or even identifying the tiny details that would matter most to clients.

3. Empathetic Negotiator: Listening more than speaking made me an empathetic negotiator. I could pick up on subtle cues, understanding what the other party truly wanted, which often led to win-win situations.

4. Trustworthiness: Clients often remarked how they felt heard and understood when they worked with me. They knew I wasn't trying to rush them into a decision for a quick sale but was genuinely looking out for their best interests.

Personal Challenges Faced

But the journey wasn't without its hiccups. Here are some challenges I faced and how I worked through them:

1. Overwhelm at Networking Events: The noise and crowd at big networking events often overwhelmed me. Instead of forcing myself to fit in, I started selecting smaller, more intimate events. When I did attend larger ones, I gave myself permission to take breaks, stepping outside for a few minutes of solitude.

2. Perceived as Uninterested: My quiet nature sometimes led clients or colleagues to think I was disinterested or aloof. To counter this, I made a conscious effort to communicate more, often recapping what I understood from conversations to show clients that I was actively engaged.

3. Fear of Missing Out: Watching extroverted colleagues seemingly effortlessly bag client after client, I sometimes felt I was missing out. However, I soon realized that my strength lay in the depth of relationships rather than the breadth. Focusing on the quality of interactions over quantity became my mantra.

In conclusion, being an introvert in the real estate industry is not a hindrance but a unique vantage point. It's about playing to your strengths, understanding your value, and navigating challenges with self-awareness. Embrace your inner introvert, and watch as doors you never imagined start opening up for you.

Chapter 2:

Building Deep Connections

In a world obsessed with "more"—more contacts, more meetings, more deals—it's easy to lose sight of the profound power of "deep." As an introvert, I've learned through personal experience that the depth of a connection often outweighs the number of connections. Let's explore the richness of building profound relationships in the real estate realm.

Quality over Quantity: Making Lasting Connections

During my initial days in real estate, I'd often find myself at large networking events, clutching a glass of drink, surrounded by a cacophony of introductions and elevator pitches. While my extroverted colleagues seemed to thrive in these environments, effortlessly flitting from one conversation to the next, I felt out of place, like a wallflower at a dance.

But over time, I recognized my strength. Instead of fleeting exchanges, I focused on a handful of individuals. Engaging in genuine conversations, I discovered their stories, aspirations, and fears. These were not just business contacts; they became relationships built on trust and understanding.

Tip: At events, instead of aiming to meet everyone, set a target. Perhaps you want to have three meaningful conversations. The depth of these connections will often prove more fruitful than dozens of superficial ones.

Listening Skills: The Introvert's Superpower in Client Relationships

I recall an instance where I was with a client, a young couple looking to buy their first home. While they listed out their requirements, I noticed a hesitation in the wife's voice when discussing the number of rooms. Instead of pushing my agenda, I paused and listened. It turned out they were planning to start a family soon, and the uncertainty of the future weighed on them. By listening actively, I could address their unspoken concerns and help find a home that catered to their present and future needs.

Introverts, by their very nature, are listeners. In the realm of real estate, this translates to:

1. Understanding Beyond Words: Clients often have concerns they might not voice outright. A keen listener can pick up on these nuances and address them proactively.

2. Building Trust: When clients feel heard, they feel valued. This fosters trust, which is the bedrock of any lasting business relationship.

3. Informed Decisions: By listening to clients, market experts, and even competitors, introverts often gather diverse insights that lead to more informed decisions.

Techniques to Engage in Genuine, Deep Conversations

Over the years, I've honed several techniques to engage more deeply during conversations:

1. Open-Ended Questions: Instead of yes-or-no questions, I often pose open-ended ones like, "How do you feel about this neighborhood?" or "What's your vision for your dream home?" These questions invite detailed answers and foster deeper engagement.

2. Silent Pauses: It's okay to let conversations have silent gaps. These moments often give both parties a chance to reflect and delve deeper into the topic.

3. Active Reflection: This involves mirroring back what you've heard, ensuring clarity and showing the speaker that you're genuinely engaged. For instance, "So, if I understand correctly, you're looking for a home with a garden because of your love for gardening."

4. Be Present: This might sound basic, but in our multitasking world, giving someone your undivided attention is a gift. Put away distractions, maintain eye contact, and immerse yourself in the conversation.

In conclusion, building deep connections in real estate—or any industry for that matter—transcends the mechanics of business. It's about recognizing the human element, understanding stories, and forging bonds that stand the test of time. Expanding on the narrative:

As introverts, we might not be the loudest voices in the room, but our ability to listen, understand, and connect on a profound level is our superpower. And in an industry where trust and understanding are paramount, this superpower is invaluable. But this journey of understanding and self-realization hasn't always been smooth for me.

I recall numerous instances in meetings where an idea or a perspective would simmer in my mind, but a deep-seated fear of judgment or ridicule would hold me back from voicing it out loud. On one such occasion, I whispered my thoughts to a colleague sitting beside me, only to watch in stunned silence as they presented the idea as their own. The room erupted in approval, and while I should've felt validated, all I felt was invisible.

This was a recurring theme, and it taught me a tough lesson about the competitive nature of commercial real estate. The phrase "dog eat dog" rang truer than ever. The sting of such experiences was further accentuated when a close friend promised to let me list his property. I was thrilled, seeing it as a golden opportunity to prove my mettle. However, my enthusiasm was short-lived. An email notification later, I was met with the cold reality that the property had been listed by another broker. It turned out his partner felt I was associated with too small a brokerage, undermining my credibility.

That experience was a turning point. I knew I needed a change, and that's when I discovered EXP Commercial. Transitioning to EXP was like stepping into a refreshing oasis after wandering in a desert. Here was a brokerage that wasn't about the relentless hustle and bustle or the sheer volume of calls and deals. They valued quality, insight, and the unique analytical skills I brought to the table. The freedom from the constant hum of cold calls and the recognition of my inherent introverted strengths was invigorating.

Being an introvert in an extroverted domain is challenging, but at EXP Commercial, I found an environment that didn't just accommodate my nature, it celebrated it. They understood that being introspective wasn't a limitation but a lens through which to view the world in greater detail. It reinforced my belief that success isn't about fitting into a mold but finding a place where your unique attributes are not just accepted but cherished.

In hindsight, the challenges, the betrayals, and the silent battles were all essential stepping stones. They made me appreciate the value of an environment that recognizes and fosters individual strengths. For fellow introverts in the real estate industry, the key is to find your tribe, an environment like EXP Commercial, where you're not bullied or sidelined for your analytical prowess but are celebrated for the depth and perspective you bring.

Remember, in a world where everyone is shouting to be heard, the quiet, reflective power of an introvert can offer the most insightful solutions. It's all about finding the right place and people who understand that.

Chapter 3:

Mastering Solo Tasks with Excellence

The world often mistakenly associates introverts with isolation, picturing them nestled in a quiet corner, engrossed in their own thoughts. But, what they fail to see is the potent combination of concentration, diligence, and profound understanding that emanates from these moments of solitude. In the real estate industry, several tasks require meticulous attention to detail, analytical prowess, and in-depth research—all of which are domains where introverts naturally excel.

Research, Analytics, and Market Knowledge: Harnessing Solitude for Success

During my early years in real estate, while many of my colleagues sought energy from group brainstorming sessions and team meetings, I discovered my rhythm in the silent corridors of market research and analytics. Here, away from the noise and distractions, I found clarity and focus.

1. Deep Dive Research: The real estate market thrives on accurate, in-depth research. Whether it's understanding neighborhood demographics, researching property

histories, or analyzing market trends, introverts, with their patience and attention to detail, can delve deeper into data, unveiling insights that might escape a cursory glance.

2. Analytical Prowess: Real estate is as much about numbers as it is about properties. Pricing strategies, return on investments, or market forecasting—all require a nuanced understanding of analytics. The introvert's ability to reflect, process, and analyze makes them naturally adept at this.

3. Continuous Learning: The real estate market is ever-evolving. An introvert's penchant for reading, studying, and upskilling ensures they remain ahead of the curve, armed with the latest market knowledge.

Capitalizing on Quiet Times: Efficiently Managing Administrative and Back-end Tasks

It was during the hushed hours of early mornings or late nights that I often found myself most productive. The world seemed to pause, granting me the serenity to tackle tasks that required undivided attention.

1. Document Management: Contracts, property listings, client communications—the administrative side of real estate can be overwhelming. But these quiet times are golden opportunities for introverts to organize, file, and manage documents efficiently.

2. Client Follow-ups: Amidst the hustle of property tours and negotiations, client follow-ups can fall through the cracks. Introverts can use their solitude to draft personalized emails or messages, ensuring clients feel valued and informed.

3. Strategic Planning: Behind every successful real estate deal is a well-thought-out strategy. Introverts can leverage their reflective nature to strategize, be it for a property sale, a marketing campaign, or client acquisition.

In conclusion, while the external world of real estate—tours, negotiations, networking—has its own charm, there's an equally important underbelly of research, analytics, and administrative tasks that keep the wheels turning. And in these domains, the introvert thrives.

By mastering solo tasks with excellence, introverts not only contribute significantly to the real estate process but also carve a niche for themselves—a space where their strengths shine, their value is undeniable, and their contributions are indispensable. It's a testament to the fact that while the industry reverberates with the sounds of negotiations and deals, it's the quiet, consistent undertones of solo tasks, managed with finesse by introverts, that lend it stability and depth.

Chapter 4:

Networking the Introvert Way

Contrary to popular belief, introverts are not anti-social or reclusive. We simply engage with the world differently, preferring meaningful one-on-one interactions over large, bustling gatherings. And when it comes to the high-energy, often extrovert-dominated sphere of networking in real estate, many introverts feel daunted. But what if I told you that networking, even for the introverted, could be not only manageable but also genuinely enjoyable?

Crafting a Networking Strategy That Feels Authentic

For introverts, authenticity is key. Rather than donning a persona that doesn't resonate, it's crucial to find a strategy that aligns with who you genuinely are.

1. Quality Over Quantity: Instead of aiming to collect numerous business cards, focus on forming a few meaningful connections. It's better to leave an event having had two in-depth conversations than twenty superficial ones.

2. Set Clear Intentions: Before attending any networking event, clarify what you aim to achieve. Whether it's to find potential clients, learn more about a particular market

segment, or simply to connect with like-minded professionals, having a clear intention can guide your interactions and make them more fulfilling.

Finding and Excelling in Low-Pressure Networking Environments

The world of networking is vast, and not every environment is a high-pressure sales pitch. Seek out platforms and venues that align with your comfort zone.

1. Special Interest Groups: Joining groups or associations related to real estate, which align with a specific interest or niche you're passionate about, can be a great way to connect. Here, the emphasis is on shared knowledge and interests, making interactions more genuine.

2. One-on-One Coffee Meets: Personalized meetings over coffee or lunch can be a great way to foster deep connections without the overwhelming stimuli of large events.

3. Webinars and Online Forums: These platforms offer opportunities to engage, ask questions, and connect in a controlled environment. You can take your time to craft thoughtful responses and engage at your own pace.

Tips for Attending Large Networking Events Without Feeling Overwhelmed

Admittedly, large networking events can be a bit much for the introverted soul. But with the right approach, they can be navigated smoothly.

1. Have an Exit Strategy: Knowing you can leave at any time can be incredibly comforting. Give yourself permission to step out for breaks or leave early if it becomes too much.

2. Buddy Up: Attend with a friend or colleague. This not only offers moral support but can also help in navigating conversations and introductions.

3. Position Yourself Strategically: Find a quiet corner or a less crowded spot where you can engage in one-on-one or small group discussions.

The Digital Advantage: Social Media as an Introvert's Networking Tool

The digital revolution has been a boon for introverts in the real estate sector. Platforms like LinkedIn, Twitter, and niche real estate forums provide an unparalleled opportunity to network without the traditional pressures.

1. Engage with Content: Sharing, commenting on, or even creating content related to real estate can establish your presence and expertise in the field.

2. DMs Over Meetings: Direct messages offer a chance to initiate conversations, discuss collaborations, or simply get to know industry peers without the immediate pressures of face-to-face interactions.

3. Virtual Networking Events: Webinars, online conferences, and virtual mixers offer the networking experience without the physical crowd. It's a space where you can listen, learn, and participate at your comfort level.

In essence, while the realm of networking in real estate might seem skewed towards the extroverted, there's ample room for introverts to not only navigate but also shine. It's about recognizing your strengths, crafting an authentic approach, and leveraging both traditional and digital platforms to build meaningful, lasting connections. Remember, in the world of real estate, genuine relationships often translate into enduring partnerships, and who better to forge such bonds than the introspective, thoughtful introvert?

Chapter 5:

Digital Real Estate – The Introvert's Playground

In an age dominated by the internet, real estate has rapidly evolved, transitioning from physical spaces to digital platforms. This shift is particularly favorable for introverts, providing avenues that align beautifully with our strengths. The digital realm offers a space where our analytical abilities, penchant for deep research, and preference for written communication can shine brightly.

Building a Powerful Online Presence

The cornerstone of succeeding in the digital age is a robust online presence. However, it's essential to approach it strategically, ensuring it reflects your authentic self.

1. Personalized Website: Consider creating a website that showcases your listings, client testimonials, and blogs or articles on real estate trends. This serves as a digital portfolio, establishing your expertise in the field.

2. SEO Optimization: Introverts often excel in tasks that require meticulous attention. Delving into the intricacies of Search Engine Optimization ensures your website ranks higher, making it easier for clients to find you.

3. Content Creation: Regularly publishing informative articles or videos helps establish you as a thought leader in real estate. Given our reflective nature, introverts often provide unique insights, making our content stand out.

Engaging with Clients on Social Media Without Draining Your Energy

Social media is an invaluable tool for networking and client engagement. However, it's essential to engage mindfully to avoid feeling overwhelmed.

1. Scheduled Posts: Use tools that allow you to schedule posts in advance. This means you can allocate specific times for social media, preventing it from becoming an incessant drain on your energy.

2. Direct Messaging: Engage with clients and prospects through DMs. This provides the intimacy of a one-on-one conversation, allowing for deeper connections.

3. Set Boundaries: Allocate specific times of the day for social media and stick to them. This ensures you remain responsive without feeling constantly tethered.

Virtual Home Tours, Webinars, and More: Making the Most of Online Tools

The digital landscape offers a plethora of tools that can revolutionize the way you operate in the real estate sector.

1. Virtual Home Tours: Leveraging technologies like 3D imaging allows you to conduct detailed property tours online. This not only saves time but also caters to international clients or those who prefer remote viewing.

2. Webinars: Hosting or participating in webinars can be a fantastic way to discuss market trends, showcase properties, or offer buying/selling tips. It's a controlled environment, perfect for introverts to share their knowledge.

3. Online Document Management: Platforms that facilitate document signing, sharing, and storage streamline the administrative side of real estate, making transactions smoother and more efficient.

In conclusion, the digital transformation of real estate is a blessing in disguise for introverts. It offers a realm where our natural inclinations—be it deep research, thoughtful content creation, or a methodical approach—become our greatest assets. By embracing the digital shift and leveraging the tools at our disposal, we can carve a niche in real estate, one that celebrates our introverted strengths while ensuring sustained success. Remember, in the vast expanse of the digital world, it's the depth, authenticity, and quality of engagement that truly makes a difference. And who better to offer that than an introvert?

Chapter 6:

Presentations and Meetings: Holding Your Ground

Let me take you back to a pivotal moment in my career. I stood at the entrance of a large conference room, my palms sweaty, heart racing. Inside, a panel of investors awaited my presentation on a new property development. As an introvert, the very idea of holding the attention of a room, navigating unexpected questions, and asserting myself in a crowd was daunting. But what I discovered that day was that, with the right preparation and mindset, I could not only manage but excel in such situations.

Preparing for Presentations: A Step-by-Step Guide

Preparation is an introvert's best friend. When you're well-prepared, half the battle is already won.

1. Know Your Material Inside-Out: Dive deep into your topic. Understand every facet of it. When you're confident in your knowledge, it radiates to your audience.

2. Rehearse, Rehearse, Rehearse: I remember standing in my living room, presenting to an imaginary panel. While it felt silly, it made me familiar with the content, flow, and timing of my presentation.

3. Anticipate Questions: Think of possible questions that could arise and prepare answers. This ensures you're not caught off-guard during Q&A sessions.

4. Use Visual Aids: Infographics, charts, or slides can be excellent tools to guide your presentation and provide visual breaks, making it easier for you to collect your thoughts.

Handling Q&A Sessions and Unexpected Turns

It was towards the end of that fateful presentation when an investor threw a curveball question. I paused, took a deep breath, and recalled my research.

1. Stay Calm: If a question surprises you, don't panic. Take a moment, gather your thoughts, and respond. It's okay to admit if you don't have an answer immediately but assure them that you'll find out.

2. Listen Actively: Often, the key to addressing a question effectively lies in understanding it thoroughly. Listen intently, and don't hesitate to ask for clarification if needed.

3. Leverage Your Introverted Strengths: Introverts excel in thoughtful, detailed responses. Use this to your advantage. Give comprehensive answers that showcase your depth of understanding.

Building Confidence in Group Settings

During another meeting, I recall feeling overshadowed by louder voices, doubting if my contributions were valuable. But over time, I've realized that it's not about volume but the value of the input.

1. Value Your Unique Perspective: Remember that as an introvert, you bring a unique perspective. Your insights, born from reflection and observation, are invaluable.

2. Practice Active Participation: Initially, I would often rehearse potential contributions in my head during meetings. It helped build my confidence to speak up.

3. Seek Feedback: After presentations or meetings, seek feedback. It not only helps you improve but also reinforces the positive aspects of your performance, boosting confidence.

4. Find Allies: Having a colleague or friend in the meeting who understands your nature can be reassuring. They can support your points or give you openings to contribute.

To my fellow introverts, I want to emphasize this: Your voice, no matter how soft or introspective, has value. In a world of cacophonous meetings and aggressive pitches, the depth, nuance, and thoughtfulness you bring to the table are indispensable. It's not about emulating the extroverts or being the loudest in the room. It's about grounding yourself in your strengths, preparing diligently, and confidently sharing your insights. The real estate world needs more of that, more of you.

Chapter 7:

Managing Stress and Preventing Burnout

It was a crisp winter morning, and I found myself staring blankly at a stack of property listings on my desk. My calendar was packed with meetings, showings, and events. Despite the whirlwind of activity, a profound sense of exhaustion enveloped me. I wasn't just physically tired; I felt emotionally and mentally drained. I had reached burnout.

As introverts, our internal reservoir of energy can deplete faster than we realize, especially in an industry as dynamic as real estate. Recognizing this and being proactive in managing stress is crucial for our well-being and success.

Recognizing Signs of Overstimulation and Fatigue

The first step to combat burnout is recognizing its early signs.

1. Decreased Motivation: You might find tasks you once approached with enthusiasm now feel burdensome.

2. Mental Fatigue: Difficulty in making decisions, forgetfulness, or a sense of mental "fogginess" can be indicators.

3. Physical Symptoms: Constant exhaustion, disrupted sleep, or frequent headaches could be warning signs.

4. Emotional Changes: Feelings of isolation, irritability, or increased sensitivity to social interactions often signal overstimulation.

Essential Self-Care Practices for Introverts

Self-care isn't a luxury; it's a necessity, especially for introverts navigating a bustling industry.

1. Scheduled Downtime: Just as you'd schedule a property viewing or a client meeting, schedule regular periods of solitude. This could be a quiet evening reading or a solo nature walk.

2. Mindfulness Practices: Engaging in activities like meditation, deep breathing exercises, or journaling can be incredibly grounding. They help center our thoughts and emotions.

3. Set Clear Boundaries: Learn to say no. Whether it's a social event after a hectic day or an additional client when you're already stretched thin, prioritize your well-being.

Balancing Solitude and Social Interactions in Your Work Week

Finding the right balance between solitude and social interactions is an art, one that's pivotal for introverts.

1. Plan Your Week Thoughtfully: If you know you have a day packed with meetings, try to keep the following day lighter. Give yourself time to recharge.

2. Leverage Technology: Make use of digital tools for tasks like initial client consultations or property briefings. Video calls or emails can sometimes replace in-person interactions, conserving your energy.

3. Designate a Sanctuary: Whether it's a corner of your home or a favorite coffee shop, have a place you can retreat to for solitude during the workday.

In the hustle of the real estate world, it's easy to get lost in the incessant demands and overlook our well-being. But remember, our introverted nature, while a tremendous asset, also necessitates vigilant self-care. Your well-being isn't just about your personal happiness; it's directly linked to your professional success. By recognizing signs of stress early, prioritizing self-care, and strategically balancing our social interactions, we can navigate this dynamic industry with vigor, enthusiasm, and resilience. Remember, it's not about the pace at which you move, but the quality and depth you bring to each step. Take care of yourself, and the rest will follow.

Chapter 8:

Forming Meaningful Partnerships

The first time I partnered with Mark, an incredibly extroverted real estate agent, I was apprehensive. Our energies were polar opposites – while I thrived in calm, reflective spaces, he was a whirlwind of enthusiasm and charisma. But as we delved into our first joint venture, a surprising revelation dawned on me: our contrasting natures, rather than being a hindrance, became our project's most significant strength.

In real estate, as in many professions, partnerships can unlock synergies that individual efforts can't match. However, for introverts, forming these connections requires understanding, mutual respect, and a keen eye for complementary skills.

Collaborating with Extroverts: A Winning Combination

The dynamics between introverts and extroverts, when channeled properly, can be potent.

1. Balanced Client Interaction: While an extrovert can engage clients with charisma and energy, introverts can forge deeper, more personal connections. A combined approach ensures that clients feel both excited and deeply understood.

2. Diverse Problem Solving: Extroverts often excel in brainstorming and quick decision-making, while introverts bring deep analysis and reflection. Together, they ensure both immediate and long-term challenges are addressed.

3. Energetic Equilibrium: In meetings or negotiations, an extroverted partner's high energy can be complemented by an introvert's calm demeanor, striking a balanced tone.

Identifying Complementary Skill Sets for Team Success

A successful partnership goes beyond personality types. It's crucial to identify skills that complement each other.

1. Client Relations: If one partner excels in initial client outreach and engagement, the other can focus on understanding client needs in-depth and ensuring long-term satisfaction.

2. Administrative Balance: An introvert's penchant for detailed, behind-the-scenes work can complement an extrovert's front-facing activities, ensuring a project's holistic success.

3. Strategic Planning: Combining the extrovert's broad, visionary thinking with the introvert's detail-oriented planning can result in robust, fail-proof strategies.

Setting Boundaries in Team Environments

While partnerships offer numerous benefits, they also require clear boundaries to ensure mutual respect and understanding.

1. Communication Protocols: Decide early on how you'll communicate – whether it's regular check-ins, weekly meetings, or written updates. As an introvert, ensure you have spaces where you can communicate comfortably.

2. Define Roles: Clearly outline who is responsible for what. This prevents overlap, ensures all aspects of a project are covered, and respects each partner's strengths.

3. Feedback Mechanisms: Constructive criticism is vital for growth. Establish a feedback mechanism where both partners feel heard and valued.

The journey with Mark taught me a priceless lesson: our differences, once understood and harnessed, became our partnership's bedrock. It wasn't about changing who we were but about embracing our unique strengths and leveraging them in unison. To all introverts looking to forge partnerships: seek balance, celebrate complementary skills, and always, always prioritize open communication. In the rich tapestry of real estate partnerships, your introverted thread has immense value – and when woven together with an extrovert's vibrant strand, the result can be truly extraordinary.

Chapter 9:

Growing Your Business Without Sacrificing Yourself

It was in my first year of real estate that I hit a wall. My business hadn't grown as significantly as I would have liked it to. but so had my exhaustion. I was constantly juggling tasks, meetings, and endless phone calls. The irony was glaring: while my business had scaled, I felt smaller than ever. The hustle was real, but was I sacrificing too much of myself in the process?

Scaling a business, especially in the competitive world of real estate, is challenging. But for introverts, the challenge often includes preserving our core energy and not losing ourselves amidst the frenzy. Here's how you can expand your enterprise without compromising your well-being.

Time Management Tips Specifically for the Introverted Real Estate Professional

Maximizing productivity while preserving energy is crucial for introverts.

1. Block Scheduling: Dedicate specific blocks of time for particular tasks. For instance, reserve mornings for research

and analysis when your mind is fresh, and afternoons for meetings when social interaction is at its peak.

2. Dedicate Quiet Hours: Set aside certain hours of your day when you don't take calls or meetings. Use this time for deep work, reflection, or simply to recharge.

3. Set Limits: Just because you can fit something into your schedule doesn't mean you should. Protect your time, and by extension, your energy.

Delegating Tasks to Maximize Your Strengths

You can't (and shouldn't) do everything on your own. Delegation is key.

1. Hire an Assistant: Even if part-time, having someone manage administrative tasks, emails, or call schedules can be freeing.

2. Leverage Technology: Use software for tasks like scheduling, reminders, or even automated follow-ups with clients. This reduces mental load and manual errors.

3. Focus on Core Strengths: Prioritize tasks that only you can do or tasks where you add the most value. Delegate the rest.

Building a Referral Network Based on Trust and Genuine Relationships

Introverts might not be schmoozers, but we excel in building authentic, lasting relationships.

1. Quality Over Quantity: Instead of trying to know everyone, focus on forging deep connections with a select group. Over time, these individuals are more likely to refer business to you out of genuine trust.

2. Follow-Up Thoughtfully: Instead of generic check-ins, send personalized notes or articles of interest. Show that you remember and value each interaction.

3. Join Introvert-Friendly Networking Groups: Not all networking has to be large, loud events. Look for smaller, more intimate groups or online forums where you can engage meaningfully.

Expansion doesn't mean mindlessly racing ahead; it means growing thoughtfully, ensuring every step aligns with your personal and professional values. As introverts, we possess the unique gift of reflection. Use it. Listen to your inner compass, delegate when needed, and always prioritize authenticity. Remember, success isn't just about numbers or size; it's about growth that feels right, resonates with your essence, and most importantly, lets you sleep peacefully at night, knowing you remained true to yourself.

Chapter 10:

Celebrating the Quiet Successes

Amidst the cacophony of ringing phones, celebratory office parties, and the loud cheers following a successful deal, there's a different kind of celebration, one that's often overlooked. It's the quiet, internal victory dance that an introverted real estate agent does when they've forged a meaningful client relationship or when they've made a well-informed decision based on hours of solitary analysis. These are the quiet successes, and they deserve recognition and celebration.

Measuring Success on Your Own Terms

Success is deeply personal and multifaceted. For introverts, it might not always be about the loudest achievements.

1. Depth Over Breadth: Maybe it's not about how many clients you have, but how deep your relationship goes with each one.

2. Knowledge and Mastery: Spending hours understanding the intricacies of the market and making informed choices can be as rewarding as any sale.

3. Personal Growth: Every time you push yourself out of your comfort zone, whether it's a presentation or a challenging negotiation, it's a success.

Testimonials: Stories from Successful Introverts in the Real Estate Industry

Sarah:"I always believed I was too 'low-energy' for real estate. But over the years, I realized that my calm demeanor put anxious homebuyers at ease. They appreciated my methodical approach and felt they could trust me. Today, I have a niche clientele who value the very traits I once doubted."

Miguel: "Networking events were nightmares for me. But instead of forcing myself into them, I started hosting small, intimate coffee sessions for clients and potential investors. These became my signature events, and my network grew organically, anchored in genuine relationships."

Looking to the Future: Continuous Growth as an Introverted Professional

The journey doesn't end; it evolves. As introverted real estate professionals, the path forward is filled with opportunities.

1. Embrace Lifelong Learning: The real estate industry, like any other, is always evolving. Dedicate time for self-education, whether it's new market trends, technologies, or personal development.

2. Seek Mentorship: Connect with other successful introverts in the industry. Their insights and experiences can be invaluable.

3. Reflect and Refine: Regularly take stock of your journey. Celebrate your successes, learn from the challenges, and set goals for the future.

As we wrap up this guide, remember: your quiet successes, though they may not always be in the spotlight, are just as significant, impactful, and worthy of celebration. The real estate world is vast and varied, with space for every kind of professional. As introverts, our strength lies in depth, authenticity, and thoughtful action. Celebrate each milestone, each achievement, and most importantly, celebrate the unique perspective and value you bring to the table. Your journey in real estate, marked by these quiet successes, is not just a testament to your professional prowess but also to the depth and richness of your character. Celebrate it, cherish it, and continue to shine in your own unique way.

Conclusion: Embracing the Journey

As we close the final pages of this guide, I find myself reflecting on my own winding journey through the intricate maze of real estate – as an introvert. The road hasn't always been easy. There were moments of doubt, hesitation, and even regret. But alongside those were triumphs, moments of clarity, and countless quiet victories that reinforced my belief in the power of authenticity.

Real estate isn't just about properties, numbers, or deals. It's about people, connections, and stories. And just as every property has its unique charm, every professional, whether introverted or extroverted, brings their own set of strengths to the table.

To you, dear reader, thank you. Thank you for sharing a part of your precious time with me. By delving into this book, you've not only embarked on a journey to understand the nuances of being an introverted professional in real estate but also embraced the narrative of someone who has walked this path, with all its ups and downs. It's my sincere hope that my stories, insights, and the collective wisdom shared here have resonated with you, offering guidance and perhaps a bit of camaraderie.

The journey of an introverted real estate professional is not a static one. It's an ongoing evolution, punctuated by moments of introspection, growth, and realization. As you continue on your path, remember that your introverted qualities are not barriers but unique strengths. They empower you to connect deeply, analyze thoughtfully, and act with purpose.

In closing, embrace your journey. Cherish the quiet successes, learn from the challenges, and always, always remain true to who you are. Here's to the roads ahead, the stories yet to be written, and the continued evolution of your unique journey in the world of real estate.

With heartfelt gratitude,

Bradley G Fagg

Appendices

A. Recommended Tools and Apps for Introverted Real Estate Professionals

1. Trello or Asana: Efficiently manage tasks, projects, and deadlines.

2. Calendly: Automate appointment scheduling without the back-and-forth.

3. Zoom: For virtual meetings and property tours.

4. Evernote: Keep notes, save articles, or jot down ideas on the go.

5. Slack or Microsoft Teams: Effective team communication without endless meetings.

6. DocuSign: Streamline the document signing process.

7. RPR (Realtors Property Resource): For market data, analytics, and client reports.

B. Script Templates

Cold Calls:

"Hello [Client's Name], this is [Your Name] from [Your Company]. I came across your property and noticed it might align with current market demands. Would you be open to a conversation about potential opportunities?"

Meetings:

"Thank you for taking the time today, [Client's Name]. I've prepared some insights that I believe would be valuable for our discussion. Let's dive in."

Negotiations:

"I understand your perspective, [Client's Name]. Let's find a middle ground that serves both our interests. Here's what I propose..."

C. Networking Groups and Communities Suited for Introverts

1. Quiet Revolution: A community focused on empowering introverts.

2. Meetup.com: Look for small, specialized real estate groups in your area.

3. BiggerPockets Forums: Engage in online real estate discussions at your own pace.

4. Toastmasters: Improve public speaking in a supportive environment.

5. Local Chamber of Commerce: Attend smaller committee meetings for more intimate networking.

About the Author:

Bradley embarked on the journey of real estate with a keen analytical mind and a preference for deeper, more meaningful interactions. Over the years, He has successfully navigated the challenges and capitalized on the strengths that come with being an introverted professional in an extroverted industry.

With a master's degree in real estate development from The University of Arizona, Bradley's expertise goes beyond mere transactional experiences. His approach to real estate is deeply rooted in understanding market intricacies, forging authentic relationships, and always prioritizing client needs.

Author's Note:

The inspiration for this book emanated from a deeply personal experience I had early in my career. At a prominent commercial brokerage, a trainer I was entrusted to made my professional journey exceptionally challenging. Unbeknownst to him, I overheard him refer to me as "lice" during a meeting I was quietly attending. He made no secret of his hopes for my failure, teaming up with another trainer to single me out, belittle me, and make me question my place in the industry.

Yet, I persevered through this training, weathering the storm of unsolicited judgments and unending challenges. Upon completion, I took a step back and parted ways with the firm, realizing there must be countless introverts in the industry who face judgment and skepticism, often from those who barely know them.

I wrote this book to champion and uplift those who are constantly underestimated, dismissed, or told they won't amount to anything. I want you to remember: believe in yourself, stay steadfast in your determination, and resist the allure of shortcuts. Real estate isn't a get-rich-quick industry; it's a realm where success is cultivated over time, demanding patience, resilience, and unwavering commitment.

But once you overcome those initial hurdles, the rewards — both personal and professional — are profound. This book is a testament to the journey and a guide for every introverted professional who believes in forging their own path, irrespective of the doubters along the way.

Legal Disclaimer

This book and its contents are intended for informational and educational purposes only. Neither the author nor the publisher shall be held responsible or liable for any losses, damages, or consequences, directly or indirectly, resulting from the use of the information provided in this work.

The strategies, tips, and anecdotes provided herein are based on the author's personal experience and opinions and should not be interpreted as specific advice or guidelines for any individual or specific situation. Readers should seek the guidance and advice of professionals, such as licensed real estate agents, brokers, or legal counsel, before making any decisions or taking actions based on the content of this book.

The real estate industry, laws, and market conditions are continually evolving. While every effort has been made to ensure that the information contained within this book is accurate and up-to-date at the time of publication, it is possible that certain aspects may become outdated or no longer applicable. It is the responsibility of the reader to verify the current status of any information, tools, or resources mentioned herein.

All trademarks, logos, and brands mentioned in this book belong to their respective owners. Their use does not imply any affiliation with or endorsement by them.

Any third-party websites, tools, or resources referenced are provided for the convenience of the reader and do not signify endorsement by the author or publisher. Users of such resources are responsible for their due diligence and discretion.

In no event shall the author, publisher, or their agents be liable to any party for any direct, indirect, special, incidental, or consequential damages, including lost profits, arising out of the use of the information contained herein, even if they have been advised of the possibility of such damages.

By reading beyond this disclaimer, readers acknowledge and agree to these terms and conditions.

www.ingramcontent.com/pod-product-compliance
Lightning Source LLC
Chambersburg PA
CBHW070609160726
48003CB00005B/2179